HANS CHRISTIAN ANDERSEN
The NIGHTINGALE

ADAPTED AND ILLUSTRATED BY
JERRY PINKNEY

McGraw Hill | SRA

Columbus, OH

SRAonline.com

 SRA

Send all inquiries to:
SRA/McGraw-Hill
4400 Easton Commons
Columbus, OH 43219-6188

ISBN: 978-0-07-612498-5
MHID: 0-07-612498-3

10 11 12 13 DRN 20 19 18 17

The McGraw·Hill Companies

To my grandchildren Rian, Victoria, and Mason

THE STORY I AM ABOUT TO TELL happened a great many years ago, so it is well to hear it now before it is forgotten. The king's palace was the most beautiful in the world. It was built entirely of the finest materials. In the garden could be seen the most unique flowers, with pretty gold bells tied to them, which jingled so that everyone who passed could not help noticing them. Indeed, everything in the king's garden was remarkable, and it extended so far that the gardener himself did not know where it ended. Those who traveled beyond its limits knew that there was a grand forest, with trees so tall they hugged the clouds, sloping down to greet the deep blue sea. In one of these trees lived a nightingale who sang so beautifully that even the poor fishermen, who had many other things to do, would stop their work and listen. "Oh, is that not splendid?" they would pronounce.

Travelers from every country in the world came to the city of the king, which they admired very much, as well as the palace and gardens; but when they heard the nightingale's song, they all declared it to be the best thing they had seen or heard. And the travelers, on their return home, related what they had found, and scholars told many stories. Books were written containing descriptions of the village, the palace, and the gardens; but they did not forget the nightingale, which was really the greatest wonder of all.

The tales traveled all over the world, and some of them came to the attention of the king; and he sat in his magnificently carved chair and listened. He nodded his approval every moment, for it pleased him to hear such admirable descriptions of his city, his palace, and his gardens. But when he heard the words "the nightingale is the most beautiful of all," he exclaimed, "What is this? I know nothing of any nightingale. Is there such a bird in my kingdom?"

Then he called one of his prime ministers, who hurried to the king's side.

"There is a very wonderful bird I hear about, called a nightingale," said the king, as he took a sip of mint tea. "They say it is the loveliest thing in my kingdom. Why have I not been told of it? It is my pleasure that she shall appear this evening at court!"

"I have never heard of her," said the minister," yet I will endeavor to find the bird."

But where was the nightingale to be found? The nobleman went through the halls and passages of the enormous palace; yet none of those whom he met had heard of the bird. So he returned to the king and said that it must only be a tale, fiction invented by those who had recited the story and those who had created the books. "Why, I even asked the magicians," he declared.

"But the talk in which I have heard this account," said the king, "was told to me by the great and mighty Truth Teller, and therefore it cannot contain a falsehood. I will hear the nightingale. She must be here this evening, and if she does not come, the whole court shall be trampled upon after supper!"

Again the prime minister ran through all the halls and corridors. Half the court ran with him, for they did not like the idea of being trampled upon. There was a great inquiry about this wonderful nightingale, whom all the world knew, but who was unknown to the court.

 At last they met with a poor little kitchen girl preparing pastries made with honey and almond milk for the king. She said, "Oh, yes, I know the nightingale quite well. Indeed, she can sing. Every evening I have permission to take home to my sick mother the scraps from the kitchen. She lives down by the seashore, and on my return I sit down in the woods to rest

and listen to the nightingales' song. Then the tears always come into my eyes, and it is just as if my mother kissed me."

"Little girl," said the king's attendant-in-waiting, "you shall have the great honor of seeing the king dine, if you will lead us to the nightingale; for she is invited this evening to the palace."

So the girl went into the woods where the nightingale sang, and half the court followed her. The forest revealed sights and sounds the likes of which the court had never seen or heard before.

"I think we shall hear her now," said the girl, and immediately the nightingale began to sing.

"Look, look! There she is."

"Is it possible?" said the king's attendant. "I never imagined it would be a little, plain, simple thing like that."

"Little nightingale," cried the girl, raising her voice, "our most gracious king wishes you to sing before him tonight."

"With the greatest pleasure," said the nightingale, and began to sing most delightfully for the girl.

"It sounds like tiny silver bells," said the prime minister. "And see how her little throat works. It is surprising that we have never heard this before; she will be a great success at court."

"My excellent nightingale," said the first courtier, "I have the pleasure of inviting you to a court festival this evening, where you will gain imperial favor from the king for your charming song."

"My song sounds best in the green woods," said the bird; but still she came willingly when she heart the king's wish.

The palace was elegantly decorated for the occasion. In the center of the great hall a golden perch had been fixed for the nightingale. The whole court was present, and the little kitchen girl watched from behind a column. All were dressed in full splendor, and every eye was turned to the little brown bird when the king nodded for her to begin. The nightingale sang so sweetly that tears came into the king's eyes, and they rolled down his cheeks as her song became still more touching and went to everyone's heart. The king was so delighted that he declared the nightingale should have his gold ring to wear around her neck, but she declined the honor with thanks.

"I have seen tears in the king's eyes," she said. "That is my richest reward. A king's tears have wonderful power, and are quite sufficient honor for me." And then she sang again more enchantingly than ever.

The nightingale's visit was most successful. She was to remain at court, to have her own cage, with freedom to go out twice a day. Servants were appointed to attend her on these occasions; each held her by a silken string fastened to her leg.

The whole city spoke of the wonderful bird, and when two people met, one said "nightin" and the other said "gale," and they understood what was meant, for nothing else was talked of.

Then one day the king received a package on which was written "The Nightingale-in-Pomp." It was a work of art contained in a small chest: an artificial nightingale, covered all over with diamonds, shells and rubies. As soon as the artificial bird was wound up, it could sing like the real one, and could move it's tail up and down, which sparkled with silver and gold.

"This is very beautiful," exclaimed all who saw it, and he who had brought the artificial bird received the title of "Imperial Nightingale-Bringer-In-Chief."

"Now they must sing together," said the court, "and what a duet it will be." But they did not get on well, for the real nightingale sang in its own natural way, while the artificial bird sang only one song.

"That is not a fault," said the music master. "It is quite perfect to my taste."

So then it sang alone, and was as successful as the real bird;
besides, it was so much prettier to look at, for it sparkled like the
stars at night. Three and thirty times did it sing the same tune with-
out being tired. The people would gladly have heard it again, but the
king said the living nightingale ought to sing something. But where
was she? No one had noticed when she flew out the open window, back to her own green woods.

"Oh, how beautiful," proclaimed the fishermen upon hearing the
nightingale's song again.

"What strange conduct," said the king when her flight had been discovered; and all the courtiers blamed her and said she was a very ungrateful creature.

"But we have the Nightingale-in-Pomp after all," said one.

The music master praised the bird in the highest degree, and even asserted that it was better then a real nightingale, not only in its carving and the beautiful diamonds, but also in its musical power. "For you must see, Your Royal Highness, that with a real nightingale we can never tell what is going to be sung, but with this bird everything is known."

Then the music master received permission to exhibit the bird to the people on the following Sunday. When they heard it, they were captivated.

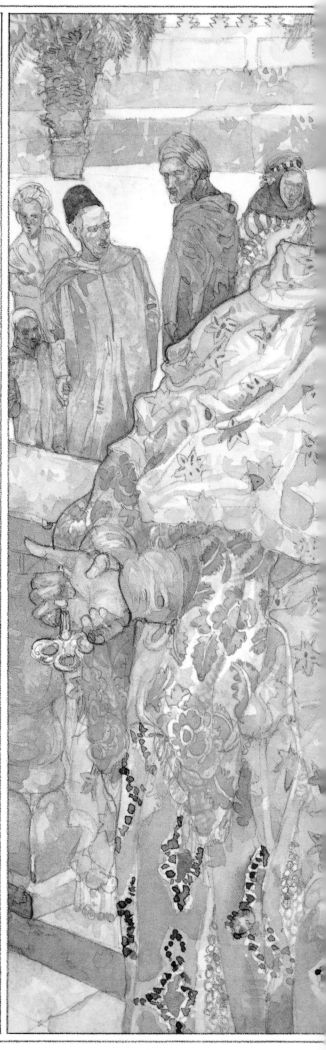

And after this, the real nightingale was banished from the kingdom, and the artificial bird placed on a woven cushion close to the king's bed. It was now advanced to the title of "Little imperial-Singer," and to the rank of Number One on the Left Hand; for the king considered the left side, on which the heart lies, as the most noble, and the heart of a king is in the same place as that of other people.

So a year passed, and the king, the court, and all the other subjects knew every little turn in the artificial bird's song; and for that same reason it pleased them better. They could sing with the bird, which they often did.

One evening, when the artificial bird was singing its best, and the king lay in bed listening, something inside the bird sounded "whizz." Then a spring cracked. "Whir-r-r-r" went all the wheels, and then the music stopped. The king immediately jumped out of bed and called for his physician; but what could he do?

Then they sent for the Great Fixer-of-All-Things. After much talking and examination, the bird was put together again. Now there was great sorrow, as the bird could only be allowed to sing on special occasions.

Five years passed, and then a real grief came upon the land. The people were quite fond of their king, and he now lay so ill that he was not expected to live. Already a new king had been chosen and the people who stood in the street asked the attendant-in-waiting how the old king was. He only lowered and shook his head.

Cold and pale lay the king in his royal bed. The whole court thought he was dying and everyone went away to welcome his successor. Carpets had been laid down on the halls and passages, so that not a footstep should be heard. A window stood open, and the moon shone in upon the king and the artificial bird.

The poor king, finding he could scarcely breathe with a strange weight on his chest, opened his eyes and saw Old Man Death sitting there. He had put on the king's golden crown, and held in one hand his sword of state and in the other his banner. All around the bed and peeping through the long woven curtains were a number of strange heads, some very ugly, and others lovely and king-looking. These were the king's good and bad deeds, which stared him in the face now that Death sat at his heart.

"Do you remember this?" "Do you recall that?" they asked one after another, thus bringing forth memories that made the perspiration stand on his brow.

"I know nothing about it," said the king. "Music! Music!" he cried. "Someone please play the bender drum, that I may not hear what they say."

But they still went on, and Old Man Death nodded to all they said.

"Music! Music!" shouted the king. "You little precious golden bird, sing, please, sing! Sing! Sing!" The Little-Imperial-Singer remained silent. There was no one to wind it up, and therefore it could not sing a note.

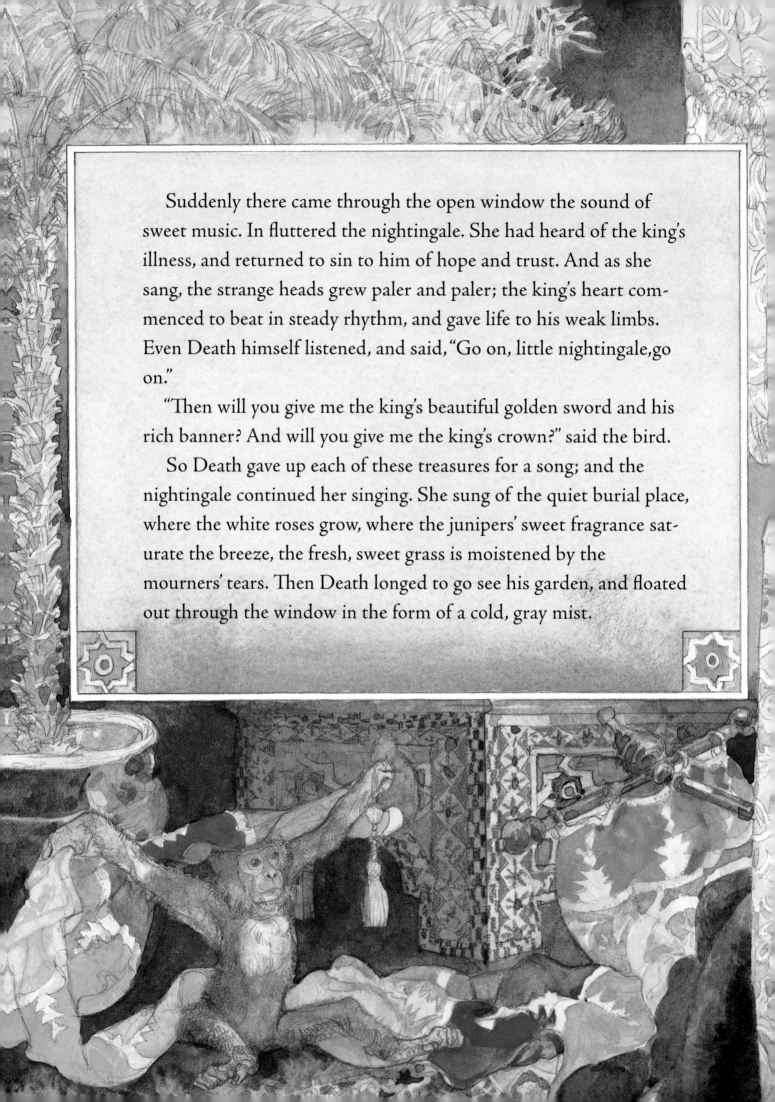

Suddenly there came through the open window the sound of sweet music. In fluttered the nightingale. She had heard of the king's illness, and returned to sin to him of hope and trust. And as she sang, the strange heads grew paler and paler; the king's heart commenced to beat in steady rhythm, and gave life to his weak limbs. Even Death himself listened, and said, "Go on, little nightingale, go on."

"Then will you give me the king's beautiful golden sword and his rich banner? And will you give me the king's crown?" said the bird.

So Death gave up each of these treasures for a song; and the nightingale continued her singing. She sung of the quiet burial place, where the white roses grow, where the junipers' sweet fragrance saturate the breeze, the fresh, sweet grass is moistened by the mourners' tears. Then Death longed to go see his garden, and floated out through the window in the form of a cold, gray mist.

"Thanks, thanks, you heavenly little bird," said the king with deep gratitude. "How can I reward you?"

"You have already rewarded me," said the nightingale. "I shall never forget that I brought tears to your eyes the first time I sang to you. These are the jewels that gladden a singer's heart. But grow strong and well. I will sing you to sleep again."

And as she sang, the king fell into a sweet slumber. When he awoke with the morning light, strengthened and rested, not one of his servants had returned. Only the nightingale still sat beside him, and sang.

"You must always remain with me," proclaimed the king. "You shall sing only when it pleases you; and I will break the artificial bird into a thousand pieces."

"No, do not do that," replied the nightingale. "The bird did very well as long as it could. I cannot live in the palace. Let me come when I like. I will sit on a limb outside your window and sing to you, so that you may be happy and have thoughts full of joy. I will sing to you of those who are fortunate and those who suffer; of the good and the evil. I love your heart better than your crown. I will come, and I will sing to you. But you must promise me one thing."

"Anything," said the king, who had dressed himself in his imperial robes.

"Promise me that you will listen to your heart, and always live in peace." So saying, the nightingale flew away.

The servants soon returned to the palace, to look after the dying king. But to their astonishment there he stood on the balcony, and looking down upon them he said, "Good morning!"

That evening a great celebration was held. The little kitchen girl was awarded an Imperial Ribbon of Honor of the highest rank. Hanging from it was a gold medallion cast in the shape of the nightingale.

IT WAS EARLY LAST SPRING when my publisher and editor, Phyllis Fogelman; art director; Atha Tehon; and I were having lunch in a lower Manhattan restaurant. We began to discuss ideas for a new adaptation of Hans Christian Andersen's fairy tale THE NIGHTINGALE. Like the original tale, all versions that we knew of were set in China. Atha proposed changing the setting to Africa. An interesting idea, I thought, but I said that I wanted to place the tale in a part of the world where one could actually find the creature.

Upon returning to my studio, I began researching the habitat of that small bird with the enchanting song. My nature library is extensive and I discovered that nightingales can be found in regions extending from Northwest Africa through Southern Europe, and from Asia Minor to Central Asia. With this knowledge the idea of placing the tale in Northwest Africa now seemed not only possible but also exciting—no other location could wrestle its way into my thought process.

I was drawn especially to Morocco because of its rich culture and racially diverse peoples who populate, share, and make their own unique contributions to that part of our world. The Moroccans, with their wide range of skin tones, as well as variety of facial features, would reflect my ideas of what is truly a society of many cultures. Also, their clothing made of fabrics of rich overlapping patterns and colors would be a challenge to my palette. The power and beauty of the country's architecture, along with its exotic landscapes, excited my imagination further.

And so, with great excitement and surrounded by books on Morocco, I began this project. After weeks of immersing myself in study, at last I was ready to enter the world of Hans Christian Andersen. The remarkable story of THE NIGHTINGALE has always intrigued me, and in the creation of this adaptation, the plain little bird with a magnificent voice and a big heart became a symbol of the healing power of nature. The little kitchen girl, who knows where the nightingale lives, became a symbol of hope for the downtrodden. And the king, who cares for his people but is out of touch with them, learns what it means to feel vulnerable through his own illness. In the end the king's recovery is made possible by two of his most humble subjects, the little kitchen girl, and the nightingale.

Jerry Pinkney